Old MUIRKIRK and Glenb

by

David Pettigrew

A milk cart ambles up a fully-developed Main Street. By the turn of the century, Muirkirk had all the amenities of the period. Gas street lighting and a regular water supply were established, as were most of the town's merchants - at that time there were 37 of them. The building housing W.S. Blackwood's general store was originally a post office belonging to John Lapraik, the poet, and was later run by the McCaul family (from 1815 to 1889). Blackwood's lasted until 1931. Another well-known Main Street firm, Trotter's, sold house-furnishings and clothing until their shop was closed in late 1995. Aside from the Co-op, Trotter's was the last of Muirkirk's large shops.

T. Johnstone's newsagents, Main Street, 1964.

INTRODUCTION

A community of less than 2000 people, Muirkirk lies in the south-east of Ayrshire amongst the hills and moors which form the edge of the Southern Uplands. Visitors to the town today may not immediately realise its significance, but Muirkirk's story is inextricably bound to the religious and industrial history of Scotland.

The first survey of the area, and the earliest recorded source of information about the parish, appears in a Charter of the Monks of Melrose in 1176. In 1565 a chapel of ease, known as 'The Kirk of the Muir' was built for the clachan of Garan - as the village was then known - by the authorities of Mauchline parish. Muirkirk parish itself came into being when it was separated from Mauchline in 1631, at which time the first parish church was built, with Garan becoming known as Moor Kirk of Kyle. Today, the only remaining artifact from the original kirk is a bell, donated around 1720 and in use there for 95 years. This can be seen in the vestibule of the present church.

The parish kirk quickly established itself as the guiding force of this unstructured community. Within two years John, Earl of Loudon, who was made patron of the parish by Parliament in 1633, had a notary's office and change-house put up in the settlement. A blacksmith, tailor, shoemaker and joiner all started businesses there in 1634, while the Earl also implemented various agricultural improvements including the building of dykes and hedges to enclose cultivated land. These developments went some way towards improving the villagers' quality of life, although they continued to endure severe hardships for decades to come. Middens stood before every door and occasionally, during very bad weather, villagers subsisted on little more than a drop of oatmeal mixed with blood drawn from their cattle. Disease and starvation were widespread, sanitation unheard of, and the rigid enforcement of religious control was a further misery to many.

During the second half of the 17th century Muirkirk occupied a significant place in Scotland's history as a centre of the Covenanters' cause. Ever since Charles I had attempted to establish an ecclesiastical policy which would assimilate practices of the Church of England with those of Scotland, religious strife had been brewing. After the distraction of the civil war, old arguments were reawakened with the Restoration. Charles II returned from exile in France to become monarch, and with his return efforts to establish his father's edicts were renewed.

When an Act of Parliament in 1662 dictated that ministers of the Kirk should be answerable to the government and the king - rather than to only the General Assembly and their parishioners – 300 of them refused to accept the legislation. Instead, they took to the hills and fields surrounding their towns where they held open-air services, or conventicles, for their supporters. In Muirkirk the effects of the Act were felt immediately when the Rev. Hugh Campbell was deposed by episcopalians within the kirk session for sympathising with the Covenanters. However, the real atrocities of the struggle didn't touch upon local areas for at least a decade. Battles for the cause were being fought in regions less remote than Muirkirk and the troubles of the outside world only entered the parish with the occasional billeting of soldiers in the kirk (where, it is reported, they were disgusted by the squalid conditions). Nevertheless, south-west Scotland held the bulwark of the support and not long after 1677, when martial law was declared in order to crush resistance once and for all, the parish was the scene of some of Scotland's most infamous brutalities.

A government army of 8000 Highlanders was sent to Ayrshire to quell the rebellions, and although largely unsuccessful in their task the soldiers treated the people they found there very harshly. Retreats for Covenanters were set up on the moors between Muirkirk and Sanquar, as well as on the farms of Burnfoot and Netherwood and also at Greenock-mains in the Wellwood area. During the last eight years of the struggle the Covenanters suffered four martyrdoms in Muirkirk. The most famous of these were the executions of the Reverend Richard Cameron and the farmer John Brown.

In 1688 the Glorious Revolution brought the Killing Times to an abrupt halt, and although the religious situation in the Parish remained unsteady until a permanent minister, the Rev. Alexander Orr, was installed in 1717, the town never experienced suffering on such a scale again. However, memories of the spilling of innocent blood were not easily erased, and various monuments to the victims and martyrs have subsequently been erected in the area. John Brown's Stone stands on the lonely site of his home on Priesthill, two miles north of Muirkirk, and his grave lies in the old kirkyard. The monument to Cameron is on Airds Moss not far west of Nether Wellwood farm, and monuments to other Covenanters are located in the town cemetery, and at Upper Wellwood and Cairntable.

After the religious troubles, the 18th century brought greater prosperity to Muirkirk. Provision for education was made in 1695, and although no proper schoolhouse was built for another 120 years the kirk session required that children be taught by local wives in the kirk meeting rooms. By 1745 markets were being held in the village three times a year where wares brought by travelling salespeople could be acquired. In the same year the first doctor arrived in Muirkirk. Villagers created their own entertainment, including rockings and penny bridals, and it was noted at the time that drunken behaviour was becoming a common problem. Agriculture finally made significant advances, with the successful introduction of sheep to the area in 1755 along with new crops of beans, wheat and pease. Nonetheless, the first half of the century was marked by serious hardship, including a lengthy period of bad weather which spoiled crops for seven years in succession. The weather was so severe in 1740 that a third of the village's population of 600 died during the winter.

During the late 18th century, Muirkirk, like many other areas of Scotland, became a focus for the activities of industrial entrepreneurs. This was prompted by the discovery in the 1780s of significant mineral reserves in the area, which led to a group of local landowners and their associates setting out to exploit the mineral wealth. The group was led by Lord Dundonald and Admiral Keith Stewart, the latter of whom bought the Wellwood Estates in 1785. Dundonald set up a tarworks in the village in 1786, and an ironworks was established there the following year. This industrialisation was responsible for a spectacular population growth in Muirkirk. The number of inhabitants increased almost five-fold from the 1740 count of 600 people, reaching 2950 in 1815. The local economy grew apace, and in the 19th century Muirkirk was one of Scotland's most important centres of industry, with its population peaking at 5000 in 1901.

Staff at Furnace Mill

But this prosperity did not last. By the mid-1920s the minerals had begun to run out, leading to a series of pit closures that drove people from the town in their hundreds to seek work elsewhere. In 1947 only 905 people were at work in Muirkirk out of a population of 4100. Within five years the total population had dropped by another thousand and the community staggered on until the final blow struck in 1968 with the closure of the last pit in the area at Kames. There have been other industries in Muirkirk over the last thirty years - mainly textile works such as Muirtex - but employment opportunities have remained scarce. Nonetheless, the town has a pioneering past to be proud of and is still surrounded today by the vestiges of its industrial heyday.

In 1631, when the parish of Muirkirk came into existence, there were only around ten dwellings in the clachan of Garan, and in 1643 its population cannot have exceeded 200 (there were 145 inhabitants aged between 16 and 60 that year). During the 17th century, the community had few resources at its disposal, and until the agricultural revolution and the establishment of the iron and mining industries a frugal existence was eked out from the largely uncultivated moorland. Garronhill is the oldest part of the town today and the original clachan lay on the southside of the Ayr - Edinburgh road. This road probably passed through the clachan at the now decaying Burnside Row, which lies at the far end of Garronhill (the opposite end to that shown in this c.1906 photograph).

Muirkirk's original church, constructed in 1631, was situated on the other side of the Edinburgh road from Garronhill. The area immediately around it was known as Kirkgreen. Of the buildings still standing there today, the row of cottages on the side dominated by the present kirk (built 1812) were probably constructed in the last twenty years of the 18th century. The cottage nearest the church on the east side of the green was built by John Loudon McAdam in 1797 and for around five years it belonged to the poet, songwriter, and friend of Burns, John Lapraik, who ran a post office and inn there until 1804. His first premises were on the present site of St Thomas' Chapel and after a period at Kirkgreen he moved to Main Street where he died in 1807. After he left, the cottage became a bank, and it is believed that a wall safe dating from the time is sealed within the right-hand room. In later years the cottage housed a bicycle shop.

The top of Main Street, c1906, with the kirk dominating the view to the east of the village. In 1772 the old kirk was in such a state of disrepair that the session agreed on its demolition and the construction of a new building. However despite having reached a decision, they procrastinated for years, only making slight improvements when absolutely necessary. But conveniently for whoever was minister at the time, they did carry out their plan to build a new manse 400 yards east of the church, and this was completed in 1801. By 1812, however, it was no longer possible to hold off the expense of a new kirk and the building was completed the following year at a cost of £1876. Work on the interior, designed to seat 1000 people (Muirkirk's population was around 2850 at the time), was not completed until July 1814, and the opening service was held that August. For a while after its replacement opened, the old kirk remained standing, perhaps because the religious masters were too stingy to pay for its demolition. However, the situation did inspire local poetess Tibbie Pagan to write one of her best known rhymes, 'The Twa Kirks'.

MAIN STREET, EAST, MUIRKIRK.

The first car arrived in Muirkirk in 1903, although for several decades afterwards it was still relatively safe for children to play in the streets. The railings on the right of the picture belong to Main Street School, built in 1815 and one of four private schools in the town at the time. Muirkirk's first school was built in 1772 by Mr Niven, owner of Tordoes estate, who donated the money for it on the condition that the school master would not be allowed to sell alcohol to the children. Originally built to replace Mr Niven's school, the Main Street building serves as the town's nursery school today.

WELLWOOD STREET, MUIRKIRK.

663 / 5

Running parallel to Main Street from Kirkgreen to Glasgow Road, Wellwood Street came into existence when these Mauchline Sandstone houses were built during the 1880s. A new church and manse was built on the corner of Wellwood Street in 1893. However, by the 1970s the church had become business premises, and in later years housed a jeans factory. This closed in 1982, and since then the building has lain neglected. In 1985, a local council survey suggested that something be done to resurrect the church building. However, eleven years later it is lying in a state of increasing dilapidation.

GLASGOW ROAD, MUIRKIRK.   663 / 13

Unlike Main Street and Furnace Road, relatively little has changed since this picture of Glasgow Road was taken roughly eighty years ago. One building was knocked down in the 1950s to make way for access to Burns Avenue, where the current local library building stands. More recently, a house which stood further up the street beside the old Chalmers Church was demolished to make way for a car park, serving the bowling green behind it. Considering the blemishes left on the town by past planning decisions, it is to the council's credit that this space was created tastefully, with the inclusion of a bench and plot of trees nearby.

FURNACE ROAD, MUIRKIRK.

663 / 6

Built in 1790, the imposing three-storey building which stood on Main Street, facing down Furnace Road, symbolised Muirkirk's new-found place as an industrial centre. The 'Great New Inn' was commissioned in response to the opening of the road to Sanquhar and in expectation of the Glasgow - Carlisle road, due to open in 1793, running through the town near the inn. With the constant flow of travellers leading to an increase in the town's size and prosperity, merchants and industrialists were anxious to exploit Muirkirk's commercial potential during the late 18th century. By 1791, its population had grown to 1500 (from 600 in 1740), with incoming workers arriving in droves and shops and small businesses springing up all along Main Street. The inn lasted for nearly 90 years. However, with the opening of the railways, coach travel through the town ceased and it closed down. After renovation the old inn became home to the manager of the ironworks, and was renamed Irondale House, although when ironworking ceased in Muirkirk the building became a doctor's surgery. It was torn down in the 1950s, and the primary school now stands on roughly the same site.

Main Street has been described, with some exaggeration, as the Princes Street of Muirkirk, 'where all the wealth and business of the town are'. As with many other towns in Scotland the Co-op in Muirkirk was - and still is - a vital asset to the community, providing almost everything that townspeople needed. Today there is one branch of the Co-op trading in Muirkirk, standing midway down Main Street across from Glasgow Road, although the building directly across the street previously belonged to the society as well (finally closing in 1976), and there were several other branches in the town. In 1926 the Co-op lent significant support to local miners during the General Strike by providing them with credit on their living needs when union support funds ran low.

By 1951 the Muirkirk Co-op had two grocery shops, a butcher's, a fruit and confection shop, a baker's, a shoe repair service, a chemist's and a draper's. 55 local people were employed and the enterprise generated a turnover of £200,000 that year. Besides expanding its operation in the town proper, the Co-op generated extra business on the southside by serving the area with vans, an opportunity that arose with the closure of Baird's general store in the late 1940s. However, this period of prosperity was relatively shortlived. As public transport to larger towns such as Kilmarnock and Ayr improved, customers travelled further afield to shops which could provide more variety than even the extensive services of the local Co-op.

Fancy Dress Parade Muirkirk. 1917.

Muirkirk's most successful public event was held in late September, 1917. The three day 'Exhibition Carnival and Fancy Dress Parade' was organised to raise money for the Red Cross and provide Christmas parcels for local men serving in France. The entire town contributed enthusiastically to the preparations, and along with visitors from all over Ayrshire they enjoyed attractions including a shooting gallery, display of war relics, performances by the Muirkirk Amateur Orchestra, and cake and game stands. But the most popular feature of the carnival was undoubtedly the invitation to beat an effigy of the Kaiser, which the crowd relished. This photograph shows the parade approaching the bottom of Glasgow Road.

Another view of the fancy dress parade, seen here passing Furnace Road School. Built around 1810 by the ironmasters for their workers' children, the school was taken over by the parish council in 1887. At the beginning of the century it was enlarged to include extra classrooms and a drill hall, and became Furnace Road Public School. Most of Muirkirk's children were educated there until it was closed in 1968 due to subsidence caused by nearby mine workings. For a year pupils were accommodated at the Main Street School and other public halls throughout the town until the modern primary school was opened on the site of Irondale House in November 1970.

The grim exterior of the E.U. Church on Glasgow Road, built in 1854 and known as the Gospel Hall. By the 1950s more than half of Muirkirk's population had lapsed from religious observance, and it was only a matter of time before only two churches remained in the town; the R.C. St Thomas' and the kirk. This picture, taken in the 1960s, illustrates the rather harsh beliefs, reminiscent of the forbidding preachings of earlier centuries, that still held sway in some congregations at the time.

The original Regal Cinema building on Main Street started life as the United Presbyterian Church hall, which was built in 1824. After being used by several churches, it became a venue for fundraising events, dances and lectures before being sold to a Mr Muir in the 1930s. He reopened the building as the Regal on 2nd December 1938, although it only survived for two months before burning down. Not defeated, however, Muir had his cinema rebuilt and the 'New Regal', shown here, opened for business in July 1939, running in competition with Willie Weir's cinema at the old Temperance Hall, also on Main Street.

SMALLBURN, MUIRKIRK.

The opening of the Regal was no doubt a major headache for Weir, who had not long beaten off the competition from Harry Caldwell's Pavilion, based in Smallburn. In 1901 this area of Muirkirk had thirty houses and a pub. By 1920 the Pavilion Cinema had opened to service what was now a substantial part of the community and Weir and Caldwell became locked in a perpetual battle for custom. The Pavilion was popular, but was notorious as a flea-pit and for the poor quality of its screenings. However, the cinemas were apparently as bad as the other. In his autobiography, Bill Shankly remembers going to one of them to see an early talkie, *The Singing Fool* with Al Jolson: 'The cinema took about six hours to show it - the film broke down about forty times and ran until 3 o'clock in the morning.'

Smallburn was the site of Muirkirk's first sports grounds, which comprised a football field, athletics track and quoiting ground. The area was levelled and prepared in 1870 by locals, who volunteered their services for free. Muirkirk football was born here and the ground first belonged to Wellwood Thistle, which became Muirkirk United in 1900. Abandoned in 1908, the ground became a slag tip, and United moved to a new site at Ladeside Park on the southside near Linkieburn Square.

As industry on the southside closed down a programme of rehousing was initiated, and during the 1930s most southsiders were relocated to brand new council housing in Smallburn. These council prefabs were erected from 1947 as an emergency measure to house the families of local men coming home from the war. They were supposed to be temporary, and consequently they left something to be desired in terms of build quality. Nonetheless, the last tenants did not leave until 1973 and for years they had to suffer cold, dampness, and the occasional loss of a roof in high winds.

Muirkirk from the Station.

With the opening of the Auchinleck-Muirkirk line of the G & S W Railway in 1848 and the Cumnock-Ayr line in 1873, Muirkirk's industrial resources were at the service of the country, and the town's economic future was secured for the next seventy years. The history of these lines was mostly uneventful. However, in 1867 wreckers, whose motives are unknown, derailed a train on Airds Moss, plunging a carriage into Welltrees Burn with the loss of two lives. The railway remained open for passenger services until 1964 and continued to be used for the transporting of coal for a further four years until heavy industry in the area came to an end.

The ironworks, c1910. Founded in 1787 by James Ewing & Co. - one year after the opening of Lord Dundonald's tarworks - they were Muirkirk's principal industrial concern until 1923, exploiting the wealth of coal and ironstone in the area. As the first ironworks in Ayrshire, they became one of the Scotland's major iron manufacturers when the railway arrived.

With their distinctive design, the furnaces at Muirkirk's ironworks, above, were known as 'the Castle'. By 1900 the works were at their peak, employing 1000 people to man the three blast furnaces. The malleable department consisted of forge and rolling mills, and the chemical works manufactured ammonia, pitch and oils from waste gases. However, sources of ironstone only lasted for a few years after the turn of the century, and despite efforts to keep the works going by processing foreign iron, they closed in 1923, leaving only the pits and the gasworks to employ the Muirkirk men. The remains of the ironworks, including the elaborate facade, were demolished in 1968.

By the early 1900s the community on the southside formed around half the population of Muirkirk as a whole. It was a tightly-knit community and noted for its neighbourliness - locked doors were unknown, as was thieving. (The southside was the scene of the only major crime in Muirkirk's history, when, in the 1890s, a miner was hanged for beating his wife to death with a poker during a drunken fit.) Although the houses were built in monotonous rows, and Park Terrace is entirely representative of this, life for the workers at that time was tolerable. The buildings, which later became dilapidated, were in a good state of repair, and Baird's, the company who owned the mines and ironworks at the time, was still providing necessary amenities for its workforce, including a shop and schooling for miners' children.

Although life was undoubtedly rough for the miners and ironworkers, their employers did contribute something towards their quality of life. The most significant of these was probably the commissioning in 1903 of an institute and church for the industrial workers of the southside. Completed in 1904, the Kames Institute had a reading room and library, function hall, games room and billiards room. There were also cloakrooms, a kitchen, baths, and a house for the caretaker. The church was demolished in December 1952, but its stained-glass window was installed in the parish kirk which was being restored after being gutted by fire in 1949. The institute still stands, and is used as an outdoor education and activity centre today. Ironworks Cottages, the single row of houses leading up to it, are virtually all that remains of the once thriving industrial community.

Bankhead Pit, near Aulhouseburn, was sunk in 1788, and with Lightshaw was one of the first pits in Muirkirk. Above are the ramshackle workings as they stood at the turn of the century.

As at all pits, the conditions at Bankhead were far from safe and in 1898 the pit flooded, killing three men. One miner, Robert Blyth, distinguished himself in rescuing many of his trapped colleagues and was awarded the Royal Humane Society's Silver Medal for his bravery. Kames Pit too was afflicted by disaster this century when an explosion in 1958 killed 19 men.

By the beginning of the 20th century the Baird management discovered that its local sources of iron ore were decreasing rapidly, and a policy of shipping ore in from Spain was introduced to maintain production. Along with the foreign ore, many Spanish and Portuguese labourers were shipped to South Ayrshire, the men finding work in local pits while their women, such as those pictured above, were given menial jobs like cleaning the pit trains. In Muirkirk the foreign labourers were housed in Linkieburn Square on the southside. Many of these immigrants died in the influenza epidemic of 1918, but descendants of the survivors are still scattered throughout Ayrshire today.

By 1915 the only pits left in Muirkirk were the two at Kames and four at Lightshaw, and of these Kames was the sole working mine in the area by 1924. Originally a single exploratory shaft sunk in 1799, this pit was not put into full production until 1870 when other local mines such as Tordoes had begun to be exhausted. As the Depression hit Britain, it was the only major industrial employer left in a town that had once been among the forefront of Ayrshire mining. In the early stages of Kames' decline, miners were given reduced working weeks to avoid redundancies, and despite early hopes that it might continue in production until at least the late 1970s Kames closed in June 1968.

Coal from Kames Colliery was transported from the pit head on spur lines to Muirkirk, from where it was forwarded to distribution depots. The Coal Board owned the spur lines and the coal was shipped on their wagons, which were connected to British Rail locomotives on the main line. To the left of this picture the Coal Board engine shed is recognisable by the section of roof raised for the ventilation of steam.

A stoker ducks to avoid the roar of his furnace at the Kames Pit. By the mid-60s, Muirkirk industry was at its lowest ebb and on the brink of extinction. The coal board had failed to stabilise mining in South Ayrshire and all over the area pits were closing, leaving thousands out of work. Those who managed to keep their jobs were not likely to have them for long, and in the meantime they regarded their work fatalistically. The dangers of the pits had always been well known, but when Muirkirk was at the peak of its industrial output the relative prosperity of the miners provided sufficient reward to compensate for these dangers. Nevertheless, the cost could be dear as one local postcard correspondent indicates: 'Uncle Jim fell in the pit going to work and cut his head…and Cousin Andrew got his face very sore burned, they don't know yet if he will lose his sight …'

When the other Muirkirk pits had closed, improvements to working conditions and efficiency at Kames were made slowly but steadily. The pit baths were built in 1933, making it no longer necessary for miners to endure the twenty minute scrub over a single bowl of water at home after work; hardly an effective remedy against the thick coal dust that caked every pore. Instead, they could have a thorough wash at the baths; something that most people would take for granted, but which the Kames miners had not had recourse to before.

More picturesque than the rows on the southside, the Bankhead miner's houses were situated near Auldhouseburn, far from the grime of the iron-works. Little has been recorded about these rows, but it is likely that they were demolished around the same time as the pit there closed. Mining returned to the area in 1950 when an open-cast operation was established there.

In 1930, Ayr County Council took over from the local parish council and began a programme of building to rehouse many of the southsiders in the main part of town. The first of these houses were completed on Middlefield Drive in 1933, although twenty years later the southside still had 1350 inhabitants. Further housing provision was made in Smallburn, and by the beginning of the sixties the rows and terraces - Linkieburn, Springhill, Midhouse - were all being demolished. As the physical gap which separated the southsiders from other Muirkirkians was reduced, the singular identity of the community was dissolved in much the same fashion as nearby Glenbuck's had been.

Furnace Road, which connected Muirkirk with the industrial southside, was at the centre of the town's development programme from earliest times. Built by McAdam as an early experiment in road construction, it was one of the first ever to use the engineer's revolutionary methods of compacting small broken stones (and here, slag from the ironworks) into a mass that was impervious to moisture. It also incorporated a camber to encourage drainage. Ironically, 'Tar' McAdam never used or promoted the use of tar in the building of roads; his nickname merely derives from his association with the tar works.

For more than a century, Muirkirk's power source was located in Furnace Road, and the buildings of the Muirkirk Coke and Gaslight Company are in the foreground of this 1964 picture. When the gasworks opened in 1859, Muirkirk become the first town in Britain to be lit by gas (electrical lighting was introduced in 1938). However, in 1977 it was the last place in Britain to be connected to the national gas network, and the works, remarkably unchanged since they first started, closed at the same time. Besides the gasworks, the last industry to be seen on Furnace Road was a dog food factory, established in the early 1970s. This short lived enterprise manufactured bone-meal, and produced such an intolerable stink that disgusted locals demanded it close.

AIRDS MILL, MUIRKIRK, W.S.S.

In 1830 a meal mill and cottage was built by the Airds family near the site of the present Mill Bridge. At that time Cottage Row stood opposite it, where Smallburn is today. Dandelion coffee was produced at the mill, amongst other things, and was very popular with the villagers. The mill closed in the 1880s and the premises were bought by the Wellwood Estate and run as a sawmill until it ceased to be operated commercially in the 1920s. The remains of the mill can be seen behind the original cottage, which is still occupied today.

When this photograph was taken, probably in the 1890s, this was the oldest house in Muirkirk. Possibly built in the mid-18th century, it belonged at one time to Tam Symington, a tea-pedlar and popular local who is likely to have occupied it until its demolition in the early years of this century. Local writer John Whyte wrote about the house in his 1926 poem, 'Tam Symington's Auld Thack Hoose'. In it, the forester's men are given blame for its destruction; an unfortunate event as Whyte considered it a building of basic but good quality: 'The ootside sae rugged,/ The inside sae douse -/ A fine cosy en'/ Was Tammy's auld hoose."

GOLF PAVILION, MUIRKIRK.

As people sought new pastimes to enliven their isolated existence, interest in sport in Muirkirk exploded in the early years of this century. Curling had been played in the local area since 1800 and this continued until the 1920s. Quoiting was also popular, and Muirkirk has had a bowling club since 1874 too. There have also been tennis and badminton facilities in the town for some time.

Muirkirk's original golf course, above, was in the Auldehouseburn area, although a new course was opened opposite Kames Institute in the 1970s.

Originally built by Lord Dundonald to facilitate the flow of traffic to and from his ironworks, the Garpel Bridge soon became known as Tibbie's Brig, a reference to one of Muirkirk's most notable characters. Isobel (Tibbie) Pagan came to Muirkirk from New Cumnock in 1755, aged 14. Although she was deeply ugly, lame and had a pronounced squint, Tibbie's character was dominated by a good-natured and creative eccentricity. A poetess and songwriter, the clever wit of her rhymes endeared her to local people, and her house by the Garpel became popular for the rockin's she held there. She was even visited by Muirkirk's gentry, who often brought guests with them to meet the celebrity. Local landowner, Admiral Keith Stewart, arranged the building of her house on the Garpel, using an old brick kiln, originally part of the tar-works, as its main structure. Although local in flavour, her work was considered good enough for publication and her book, *Songs and Poems On Several Occasions,* appeared in 1803. A copy is now held by the British Museum.

Tibbie died in 1821 and was buried in the old Kirkyard between John Brown the covenanter and John Lapraik. A commemorative monument was built on the site of her home near the brig on the centenary of her death. Always a favourite spot for picnics, the picture above shows the brig on a summer's day in the 1950s with groups of swimmers and sunbathers enjoying a rare spell of warm weather - note the swimming hole to the right of the tree. In August 1995 the brig was repaired and restored it to its original condition, after fears that it may collapse. However, some local people have expressed their regret that restoration has left little of its former rustic charm.

The most historically significant house in Muirkirk, Auldhouseburn was built in 1610 and was once a hide-out for Covenanters. At one time an underground tunnel, used by the men, led from the basement to the moors beyond. Two of the most famous of Muirkirk's martyrs from this period are Richard Cameron, who was killed in a battle with government troops on Airds Moss in 1680; and John Brown, shot in front of his family by Grahame of Claverhouse in 1685. Random acts of violence in Muirkirk reached an alarming intensity around the time of the Covenanters, with 82 people killed in the parish in only two years between 1684 and 1686. Auldhouseburn was rebuilt in 1884 and is still occupied today.

Several lavish country houses were built during the height of Muirkirk's industrial prosperity to accommodate the town's various ironmasters and pit managers. The first of these was Springhill House, situated close to the British Tar Company works. The works were established in 1786 by Lord Dundonald, to exploit his patents for producing tar, lampblack and varnish from coal, and were near the present Kames Outdoor Centre. Their establishment marked the beginning of industrialisation in Muirkirk and the works were instrumental in bringing the area to the attention of other businessmen. Springhill House was built for the tarworks' manager, Alexander Cochrane, and later became the home of John McAdam when he took over the operation. Although the exact date of its demolition is unknown, the ruins of Springhill can still be seen, as can the nearby cairn commemorating McAdam and the tarworks which closed in 1827.

Wellwood House was the residence of J.G.A. Baird, M.P. One of the oldest houses in the area, it was built in 1600 and extended twice in 1740 and 1878. Who the original owners were, and why they chose to build the house are unknown, but a spectre from that period, the ghost of a murdered young woman called Beenie, was said to haunt the building and its grounds. Beenie was reputedly often seen weeping amongst the trees in the grounds, and residents never slept in a particular bedroom as the stairway leading to it was supposed to be regularly marked by bloodstains which always reappeared despite being scrubbed off. Finally, a mason was called to replace the step on which the blood appeared and within hours of completing the job he died from unknown causes. The ghost of Beenie has not been seen since the house was demolished in 1928.

The most attractive of the local large houses was Glenbuck House, situated at today's Glenbuck Home Farm, where the lodge is still occupied. Erected in 1880 for the Laird of Glenbuck, Charles Howatson, its baronial design suitably illustrates the ostentatious wealth of this self-made man, whose principal fame arose from his breeding of hardy black-faced sheep. At the time such landowners no doubt believed that their descendants would dominate the area for hundreds of years to come, but it was not to be. Howatson died and his family moved away leaving the house condemned to demolition in 1948. For many years, however, the black-faced sheep remained, grazing the grasses spread through time over the ruins of their breeder's house.

GLENBUCK

"Life was not easy in the village when we were growing up. No disrespect to Glenbuck, but you could have been as far away from civilisation in Outer Mongolia. The winters were cold and bitter with four months of snow."

- Bill Shankly, Shankly on Shankly

Around three miles east of Muirkirk, on a turn-off from the A70, lie the fast disappearing ruins of Glenbuck. Like the southside of Muirkirk this village has died with its industry, and today there are only three inhabited buildings, only one of which lies over the mouldering stones of the village centre.

When the Douglas family's influence in Scottish affairs was at its height in the late 14th and early 15th century, the area to the east of Muirkirk formed part of their hunting grounds. Known as Buck Glen, it must have been rich in deer then. However, the extent and thoroughness of their culls was such that the land was stripped of trees and wildlife; having been left desolate, it remained uninhabited for perhaps another 200 years.

Although Glenbuck grew considerably as a direct consequence of the discovery of its mineral wealth, it is difficult to understand why people settled there in the first place, as the minerals were only discovered 100 years after its establishment. Situated on much higher ground than Muirkirk, the isolation of the area - particularly in winter, as Shankly points out - has always been extreme. Possibly the search for easily dug coal brought people there, or perhaps the mistaken belief that the land would yield better crops than that of Muirkirk. What is known is that habitation had not arrived by 1631, when Muirkirk separated from Mauchline, and did not appear until 1650 when a settlement of around 40 people had established itself. There was probably no livestock, and farming would have been a primitive battle with the moors; these people, as in Muirkirk, barely surviving on what they could wrench from the muddy bog.

For Glenbuck, recorded history began in earnest with the arrival of industry in 1760, when the New Mills Weaving Company of Lanark opened a short-lived factory there. The benefits, albeit small, were immediately felt and two years later the population had reached 580. Agricultural matters also improved and by 1770 seven new farm holdings appeared in the immediate vicinity.

When Muirkirk was assessed for mineral wealth in the early 1780s Glenbuck was also investigated, and as a result the Cairntable Gas & Coal Company established a small mine and ironworks there. Like Muirkirk, Glenbuck enjoyed a rapid expansion in population and prosperity and by 1800 there were 800 people in the village. The 19th century saw the coming of the railway and to a certain extent the isolation of the past disappeared. However, it was not a place many came to visit and the community became extremely tight-knit. The best example of the pride and loyalties of the people is illustrated by its fierce support of local football teams. The famous Cherrypickers hailed from Glenbuck and their matches were fraught with rivalry and bad feeling. It was not unusual for players of opposing teams to be pelted by stones and the presence of a policeman was often required, if only to perform no more serious a duty than fishing an unpopular referee out of a nearby pond.

By 1900 Glenbuck's population had reached 1750, but at the same time began a decline similar to the one that Muirkirk was experiencing simultaneously. From 1908 onwards the pits began to close, and in only 14 years the population had dropped to 700. When the last pit, Grasshill, shut in 1933 the village's dereliction was assured and by the fifties the population had melted away almost completely. A few continued to live there right into the seventies, but with their departure Glenbuck became an empty spot on the map.

Parish Church and War Memorial, Glenbuck.

The west end of Glenbuck's Main Street. Housing in the village was made up of rows, including Jubilee, Spireslack, and Grasshill. So complete has been the demise of Glenbuck, that nowadays it is virtually impossible to get any detailed information on the village. Places such as Kerr's Buildings (possibly an early community centre), the Auchenshilloch Cottages and the Castle are now nothing more than just names.

For the young people of Glenbuck, with no wireless, cinema, or transport to better places, the main source of diversion came in the shape of a football. However, Glenbuck, perhaps in greater need of diversion than most other towns, embraced the sport with particular passion. Its tradition of junior football fostered more professional players of outstanding ability than any other village club of its time, and Glenbuck was known as the 'Nursery of Footballers'. Glenbuck Athletic was formed in the late 1870s by Edward Bone and William Brown to exploit the talent already evident on the scraps of wasteground around the village where the young lads played. Team members were not only unpaid, but also expected to subsidise the privilege of playing by providing their own strip, paying their own expenses and contributing a shilling a week for the upkeep of the ground. When a pit shaft was sunk through it, Glenbuck's team lost their ground, moving to a hillside overlooking the village, and finally to Burnside Park (above) where they made their name.

48

GLENBUCK CHERRYPICKERS

At the turn of the century Glenbuck's team became known as the Cherrypickers. The origin of this name is unknown, but is credited to various stories, including one concerning the scandalous theft of a basket of cherries from Miliken's Store by members of the team. In the years before the First World War the Cherrypickers notched up an impressive number of victories, winning no less than 11 Ayrshire trophies before 1914. They produced an unprecedented 50 players who went on to careers in professional football, 37 of them progressing to the English leagues or in one case to a team in the U.S.A., and 7 of them representing Scotland. The most famous of these players were undoubtedly the five Shankly brothers who represented between them ten clubs throughout Britain; Robert and Bill going on to become managers. Bill played for Preston North End and Carlisle, and was capped for Scotland thirteen times, before beginning a managerial career with Grimsby Town. As manager of Liverpool in the 1970s he attained the status of legend, his team becoming several times F.A., League, and European champions throughout that decade.

Glenbuck would not have been a fully-fledged town without a Co-op, and as in Muirkirk the population relied greatly on its services. However, it was not the only store and faced competition from Bain's fruit shop, Miss Kerr's drapery, Bob Lang the tailor and Hamilton's butcher shop. There were also two sweet shops, a fish & chip shop and, most importantly, the Royal Arms public house.

Despite the pit closures, Glenbuck continued to survive for over twenty years, and small industries such as knitwear and finishing factories came and went. By 1951 there were still 320 inhabitants but conditions were poor. 86 of the 107 houses were condemned, the water supply was threatened in dry weather and there were only 16 baths in the whole place. In 1952 the railway to Coalburn was closed. For a few years since the late forties reunions of villagers who had moved away took place annually in Glenbuck, but by 1954 this seemed a pointless practice. Nearly everybody had left, the isolation of pre-rail days had returned, and with no industry of any sort there was little else for the town to do but disappear into the past.

Muirkirk Station, 1964.